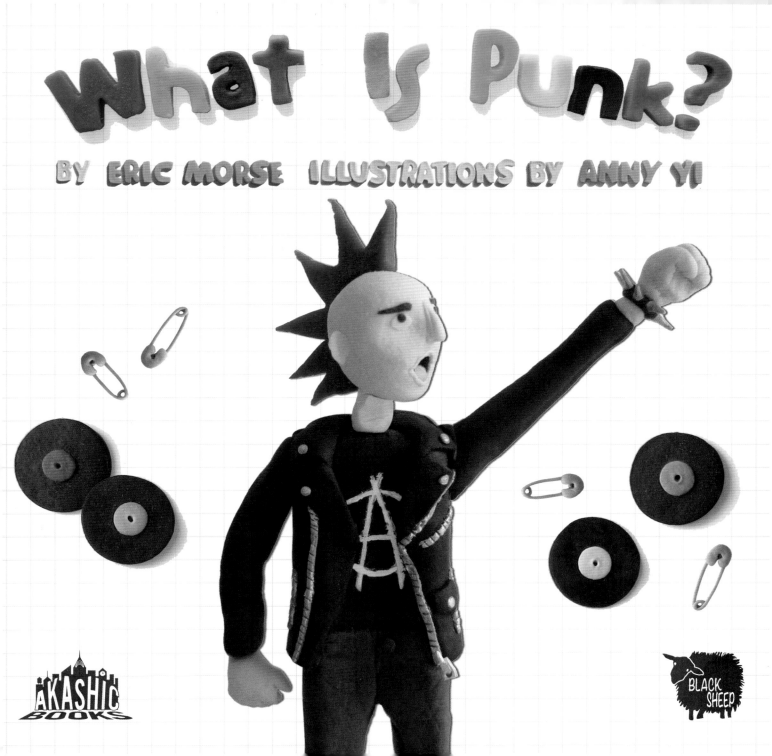

What Is Punk?

BY ERIC MORSE ILLUSTRATIONS BY ANNY YI

Published by Black Sheep/
Akashic Books

Twitter: @akashicbooks

Facebook: akashicbooks

info@akashicbooks

www.akashicbooks.com

ISBN: 978-1-61775-392-3
Library of Congress Control Number: 2015933858
First printing

Once upon a time,
there was a deafening roar,
that awakened the people,
like never before.

With their eyes open wide
they shouted in fear,
"What new sound is this?"
and covered their ears.

IT WAS

So what is this "punk"?
you may want to know.
Are there *people* called punks?
Did *they* make it so?

Did punk come from here,
or way over there?
Rise up from the dirt,
spring out of thin air?

Some think punk was born in downtown New York City, with a sonic revolution at Max's and CBGB.

Tom Verlaine of Television

Debbie Harry of Blondie

David Byrne of Talking Heads

Kids jumped out of their seats,
started climbing the walls,
for the music of Television
and the New York Dolls.

There were Talking Heads too,
and the Velvet Underground,
and the fierce band Blondie,
all with a fresh new sound.

David Johansen
of the New York Dolls

Lou Reed
of the Velvet Undgergound

From the borough of Queens
came contenders to the throne:
in blue jeans and leather,
four teens called RAMONES.

GABBA GABBA HEY

They got straight to the point:
a one, a two, and three four,
"Hey ho, let's go,"
two-minute songs—never more.

Out near Lake Michigan,
where they build America's cars,
Motown funk met gritty punk—
and Detroit had a new star.

Iggy Pop and the Stooges
were known for outrageous stunts.
If you ask, anyone will tell you:
Iggy never wore a shirt, not once!

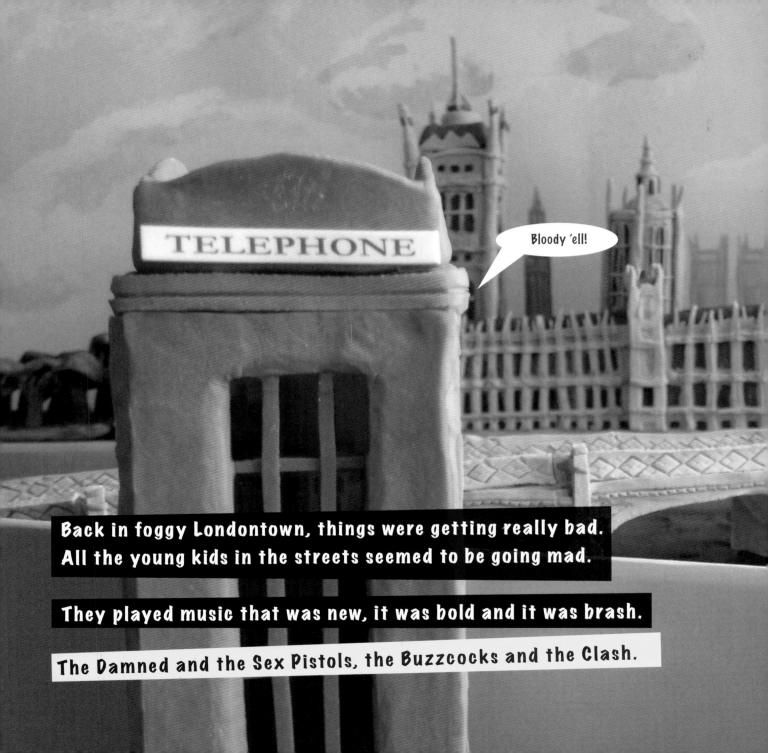

That's right, the Sex Pistols—
a name naughty as can be—
would harass the upper class,
with songs of Queen and anarchy.

They hoped that their sound would never be forgotten. So they made up silly names like Sid Vicious and John Rotten.
THE U.K.

And when London was burning,
the mighty CLASH heard the call.
They played songs for working people
and equality for all.

When the Clash "fought the law,"
they were the coolest band around!
With their punk rock and ska,
they defined a brand-new sound.

The Slits

Punks made a lot of noise,
they had something to say.
And just like the boys,
the girls came to play.

Siouxsie, Go-Gos, and Blondie,
X-Ray Spex and the Slits
all made a holy racket
with their glitter and their grit.

Poly Styrene
of X-Ray Spex

Siouxsie Sioux

Out West in sunny LA, they live close to the beach.
Bands like X and Black Flag had a punk gospel to preach.

Keith Morris

The Germs

Circle Jerks

The Descendents and the Dickies, Circle Jerks, Germs, and Weirdos, were all punks who had fun and kept fans on their toes.

Henry Rollins

Descendents

In Washington, DC,
Bad Brains were the rage.
They played reggae and hardcore
and brought on punk's new age.

They say punk is a sound,
it can be loud and fast.
But it's also a movement—
ask the Misfits, ask Crass.

PUNK
STREET

In your city or town, you'll find many more stories of punk culture to learn and explore.

ZINES

So what is this punk,
you still want to know?
Is it noise or just junk?
Did it die long ago?

Punk is music, it's art,
it's culture and vision.
But if you really want to know punk . . .

You just have to LISTEN.